Jan wanted a new anorak.

She went to the shop.

She liked this anorak.

Jan wore her new anorak.

She went to play.

It was hot.

Jan put her anorak down.

She played on the swing.

Jan couldn't see her anorak.

A girl had it.

Jan wanted her anorak.

She pulled it off the girl.

The anorak was too big.

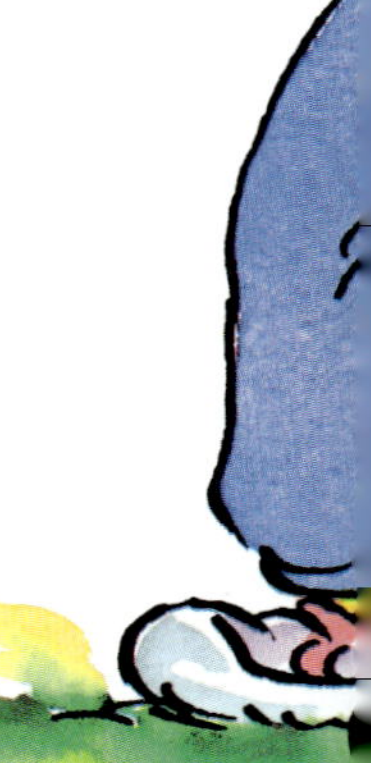

'Oh no!' said Jan.

Jan's mum had her anorak.
'Sorry,' said Jan.